I Could Be...

Susanna Kendall

When I've been being me all day
From breakfast time till tea,

I sometimes stop and wonder
Just who I'd like to be.

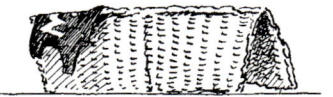

I could be a speedy sprinter
Running all the races.

I could be a funny clown
Who's always making faces.

I could be a gardener
Growing strawberries for tea.

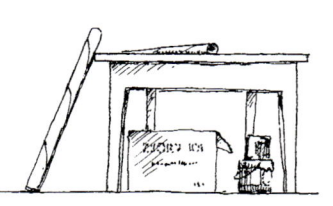

I could be a lighthouse keeper
Looking out to sea.

I could be a builder
Laying bricks to make a wall,

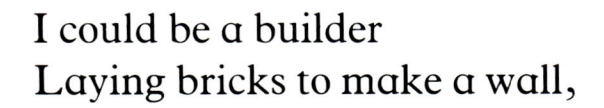

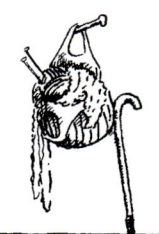

Or an octogenarian
Who knits himself a shawl.

I could fly an aeroplane
and loop the loop with ease,

.... or I could have a CAFE

and serve

Or I could have a cafe
And serve breakfasts, lunches, teas.

I could be the fiddler
Who makes all the people dance,

Or I could be a cyclist
Who rides all the way round France.

But when I really wonder
Just who I'd like to be,